The Everlasting Gospel

& Other Poems

by William Blake

edited by Sasha Newborn

BΔNDΔNNΔ BOOKS 2011 SΔNTΔ BΔRBΔRΔ

BANDANNA BOOKS COLLEGE TITLES

SAPPHO: THE POEMS.* $9.95

AREOPAGITICA: FREEDOM OF THE PRESS.* John Milton.

APOLOGY OF SOCRATES, & THE CRITO.* Plato.

THE FIRST DETECTIVE: THREE STORIES. EDGAR ALLAN POE.
    Murders in Rue Morgue, Purloined Letter

DON'T PANIC: THE PROCRASTINATOR'S GUIDE TO
    WRITING AN EFFECTIVE TERM PAPER.

MITOS Y LEYENDAS DE MÉXICO/MYTHS AND LEGENDS OF MEXICO.
    Luis Leal. Bilingual. Color plates

GHAZALS OF GHALIB. Ghalib argues with God

THE MERCHANT OF VENICE. William Shakespeare. Orson Welles

GANDHI ON THE GITA. Explained chapter by chapter.

LEAVES OF GRASS, Original edition.¹
    Walt Whitman.

ITALIAN FOR OPERA LOVERS. Italian opera term

DANTE & HIS CIRCLE. The young Dante with a dozen poets

Vita Nuova. Dante Alighieri

*Teacher supplements available.

PREFACE

BLAKE'S NOTEBOOKS after his death disclose an unfinished poem titled "The Everlasting Gospel" present in about a dozen pieces, and indications of at least one more version that is missing. Several pieces are rewrites (sections 1 and 3), some are obvious inserts or unattached couplets. No arrangement is recognized as standard, and this edition is no exception.

Yet the message of the poem is enduring, and presents a humanist document with few parallels and perhaps no predecessors. Blake's personality was seen by his contemporaries as part genius, part naïf —just the combination to touch areas of sensibility remote from the rest of us. But, in fact, good and evil are not at all remote, they are simply removed from our daily considerations. To live with such consciousness, and with such conviction to shout against the platitudes of our lives, may be possible only for such a personality. Blake's ability to step outside the conventional thinking of his day (and of ours) gave him a point of view from which he could critically re-evaluate cherished values and expectations of the Christian tradition, such as good and evil.

The very short pieces entitled "There Is No Natural Religion" and "All Religions Are One" were both published in 1788, when Blake was thirty-one, and "The Marriage of Heaven and Hell" was written not long after. The fragments of "The Everlasting Gospel" are variously dated from 1808 to 1818, at which time Blake was in his fifties. It was never published in Blake's lifetime.

This text has been modernized where practicable, replacing antiquated usages such as *thee* and *thine* with *you* and *your*. More problematic in editing for modern readers is Blake's use of "man" or "men" to describe humanity. In his visual art, Blake portrays men and women with a clear eye, but, fair warning: his language is not as equitable.

Blake's approach to the teaching of Jesus is uniquely his own, not representing any recognized Christian dogma. He argues with Swedenborg in a friendly way, for both of them saw visions—just not the same ones.

I understand these pieces to be his best effort at talking to people who did not share the spiritual depth that he experienced. May these messages speak to you.

Sasha Newborn
September 2011

CONTENTS

THE EVERLASTING GOSPEL

There is not one moral virtue that Jesus inculcated
but Plato and Cicero did inculcate before him.
What then did Christ inculcate? Forgiveness of
Sins. This alone is the gospel and this is the life
and immortality brought to light by Jesus. Even the
covenant of Jehovah, which is this: If you forgive
one another your trespasses, so shall Jehovah forgive
you, That he himself may dwell among you, but if
you avenge, you murder the divine image and he
cannot dwell among you because you murder him.
He arises again and you deny that he is arisen and
are blind to spirit.

If Moral Virtue was christianity,
Christ's pretensions were all vanity;
and Caiaphas and Pilate men
praiseworthy, and the lion's den
and not the sheepfold allegories
of God and Heaven and their glories.
The moral christian is the cause
of the unbeliever and his/her laws;
the Roman virtues, warlike fame,
take Jesus' and Jehovah's name,
for what is antichrist but those
who against sinners Heaven close
with iron bars, in virtuous state
and Rhadamanthus at the gate?

§

The vision of Christ that you do see
is my vision's greatest enemy;
yours has a great hook nose like you,
mine has a snub nose like to mine;
yours is the friend of all humankind,
mine speaks in parables to the blind.
Yours loves the same world that mine hates;
your Heaven doors are my Hell gates.
Socrates taught what Melitus
loathed as a nation's bitterest curse;
and Caiaphas was in his own mind
a benefactor to humankind.
Both read the Bible day and night,
but you read black where I read white.

§

What can this gospel of Jesus be?
What life and immortality?
What was it that he brought to light
that Plato and Cicero did not write?
The heathen deities wrote them all,
these moral virtues great and small.
What is the accusation of sin
but moral virtues' deadly gin?
The moral virtues in their pride
did over the world triumphant ride
in wars and sacrifice for sin,
and souls to Hell ran trooping in.
The accuser, holy god of all
this pharisaic worldly ball,
amidst them in whose glory beams
upon the rivers and the streams.
Then Jesus rose and said to me,
"Your sins are all forgiven you."
Loud Pilate howled, loud Caiaphas yelled
when they the gospel light beheld.
It was when Jesus said to me,

"Your sins are all forgiven you."
The Christian trumpets loud proclaim
through all the world in Jesus' name
mutual forgiveness of each vice
and opened the gates of Paradise.
The moral virtues in great fear
formed the cross and nails and spear,
and the accuser standing by
cried out, "Crucify, crucify!"
Our mortal virtues never can be
nor warlike pomp and majesty,
for moral virtues all begin
in the accusations of sin
and all the heroic virtues end
in destroying the sinner's friend.
"Am I not Lucifer the great?
And you my daughters in great state,
the fruit of my mysterious tree
of good and evil and misery
and death and Hell, which now begin
on everyone who forgives sin?"

§

Seeing this false Christ, in fury and passion
I made my voice heard all over the nation.

§

THE EVERLASTING GOSPEL

Was Jesus humble or did he
give any proofs of humility?
Boast of high things with humble tone
and give with charity a stone?
When but a child he ran away
and left his parents in dismay.
When they had wandered three days long
these were the words upon his tongue:
"No earthly parents I confess,
I am doing my Father's business."
When the rich learned Pharisee
came to consult him secretly,
upon his heart with iron pen
he wrote, "You must be born again."

He was too proud to take a bribe;
he spoke with authority, not like a scribe.
He says with most consummate art,
"Follow me, I am meek and lowly of heart,"
as that is the only way to escape
the miser's net and the glutton's trap.
What can be done with such desperate fools
who follow after the heathen schools?
I was standing by when Jesus died;
what I called humility, they called pride.
One who loves one's enemies betrays one's friends;
this surely is not what Jesus intends,
but the sneaking pride of heroic schools,
and the Scribes' and Pharisees' virtuous rules
for he acts with honest, triumphant pride,
and this is the cause that Jesus died.
He did not die with Christian ease,
asking pardon of his enemies:

if he had, Caiaphas would forgive;
sneaking submission can always live.
He had only to say that God was the devil,
and the devil was God, like a Christian civil.
Mild Christian regrets to the Devil confess
for affronting him thrice in the wilderness.
Like Dr. Priestley and Bacon and Newton,
poor spiritual knowledge is not worth a button!
He had soon been bloody Caesar's Elf,
and at last he would have been Caesar himself.
For thus the gospel Sir Isaac confutes:
"God can only be known by His attributes;
and as for the indwelling of the Holy Ghost
or of Christ and his Father, it's all a boast,
and pride and vanity of the imagination
that disdains to follow this world's fashion."
To teach doubt and experiment
certainly was not what Christ meant.

What was he doing all that time
from twelve years old to manly prime?
Was he then idle, or the less
about his Father's business,
or was his wisdom held in scorn
before his wrath began to burn
in miracles throughout the land
that quite unnerved Caiaphas' hand?
If he had been Antichrist, creeping Jesus,
he'd have done anything to please us:
gone sneaking into synagogues
and not used the elders and priests like dogs,
but humble as a lamb or ass
obeyed himself to Caiaphas.

God wants not men to humble themselves;
This is the trick of the ancient Elf.
This is the race that Jesus ran:
humble to God, haughty to man,
cursing the rulers before the people
even to the temple's highest steeple;
and when he humbled himself to God
then descended the cruel rod:
"If you humble yourself, you humble me;
you also dwell in eternity.
You are a man, God is no more;
your own humanity learn to adore,
for that is my spirit of life.
Awake, arise to spiritual strife

and your revenge abroad display
in terrors at the Last Judgment day;
God's mercy and long suffering
is but the sinner to judgment to bring.
You on the cross for them shall pray
and take revenge at the Last Day."

Jesus replied and thunders hurled,
"I never will pray for the world!
Once I did so when I prayed in the garden;
I wished to take with me a bodily pardon."
Can that which was of woman born
in the absence of the morn
when the soul fell into sleep—
and archangels round it weep—

shooting out against the light
fibers of a deadly night,
reasoning upon its own dark fiction
in doubt which is self contradiction?
Humility is only doubt.
And does the sun and moon blot out,
rooting over with thorns and stems
the buried soul and all its gems.
This life's dim windows of the soul
distorts the heavens from pole to pole
and leads you to believe a lie
when you see with, not through, the eye
that was born in a night to perish in a night
when the soul slept in the beams of light.

§

§

Was Jesus chaste? or did he
give any lessons of chastity?
The morning blushed fiery red;
Mary was found in adulterous bed.
Earth groaned beneath and Heaven above
trembled at discovery of love.
Jesus was sitting in Moses' chair;
they brought the trembling woman there.
Moses commands she be stoned to death.
What was the sound of Jesus' breath?
He laid his hand on Moses' law;
the ancient heavens in silent awe
writ with curses from pole to pole
all away began to roll.
The earth trembling and naked lay
in secret bed of mortal clay,

on Sinai felt the hand divine
putting back the bloody shrine,
and she heard the breath of God,
as she heard by Eden's flood:
"Good and evil are no more!
Sinai's trumpets cease to roar!
Cease, finger of God, to write!
The heavens are not clean in your sight!
You are good and you alone,
nor may the sinner cast one stone.
To be good only is to be
A god/devil or else a Pharisee.
You angel of the presence divine
that did create this body of mine,
wherefore have you writ these laws
and created Hell's dark jaws?

My presence I will take from you;
a cold leper you shall be.
Though you were so pure and bright
that Heaven was impure in your sight,
though your oath turned Heaven pale,
though your covenant built Hell's jail,
though you did all to chaos roll
with the serpent for its soul,
still the breath divine does move
and the breath divine is love.
Mary, fear not, let me see
the seven devils that torment you.
Hide not from my sight your sin
that forgiveness you may win.

Has no one condemned you?"
"No one, Lord!" "Then what is one who
shall accuse you?—Come you forth,
fallen fiends of heavenly birth
that have forgot your ancient love
and driven away my trembling dove!
You shall bow before her feet;
you shall lick the dust for meat;
and though you cannot love, but hate,
shall be beggars at Love's gate.
What was your love? Let me see it:
was it love or dark deceit?"
"Love too long from me has fled.
'Twas dark deceit to earn my bread;

'twas covet, or 'twas custom, or
some trifle not worth caring for,
that they may call a shame and sin
Love's temple that God dwells in,
and hide in secret hidden shrine
the naked human form divine,
and render that a lawless thing
on which the soul expands its wing.
But this, O Lord, this was my sin:
when first I let these devils in,
in dark pretence to chastity,
blaspheming love, blaspheming you.
Thence rose secret adulteries
and thence did covet also rise.
My sin you have forgiven me,
can you forgive my blasphemy?
Can you return to this dark Hell
and in my burning bosom dwell?

And can you die that I may live,
and can you pity and forgive?"
Then rolled the shadowy man away
from the limbs of Jesus to make them whose prey—
an ever-devouring appetite,
glittering with festering venoms bright—
crying, "Crucify this cause of distress
who don't keep the secrets of holiness!
All mental powers by diseases we bind,
but he heals the deaf and the dumb and the blind.
Whom God has afflicted for secret ends
he comforts and heals and calls them friends."
But when Jesus was crucified
then was perfected his glittering pride;
in three nights he devoured his prey,
and still he devours the body of clay,
for dust and clay is the serpent's meat
which never was made for Humanity to eat.

§

§

Was Jesus gentle or did he
give any marks of gentility?
When twelve years old he ran away
and left his parents in dismay.
When after three days' sorrow found,
loud as Sinai's trumpet sound:
"No earthly parents, I confess
my heavenly Father's business!
You understand not what I say,
and, angry, force me to obey."
Obedience is a duty then,
and favor gains with God and men.

John from the wilderness loud cried,
Satan gloried in his pride.
"Come," said Satan, "come away.
I'll soon see if you'll obey!

John for disobedience bled,
but you can turn the stones to bread.
God's high king and God's high priest
shall plant their glories in your breast
if Caiaphas you will obey,
if Herod you with bloody prey
feed with the sacrifice, and be
obedient. Fall down and worship me!"
Thunders and lightnings broke around
and Jesus' voice in thunders sound:
"Thus I seize the spiritual prey!
You smiters with disease, make way.
I come your king and god to seize.
Is God a smiter with disease?"
The God of this world raged in vain.
He bound old Satan in his chain
and bursting forth, his furious ire
became a chariot of fire.

Throughout the land he took his course
and traced diseases to their source;
he cursed the Scribe and Pharisee,
trampling down hypocrisy.
Wherever his chariot took its way,
there gates of death let in the day,
broke down from every chain and bar.
And Satan in whose spiritual war
dragged at his chariot wheels; loud howled
the god of this world; louder rolled
the chariot wheels; and louder still
his voice was heard from Zion's hill.
And in his hand the scourge shone bright;
he scourged the merchant Canaanite

from out the temple of his mind,
and in his body tight does bind
Satan and all whose hellish Crew.
And thus with wrath he did subdue
the serpent bulk of Nature's dross
till he had nailed it to the cross.
He took on sin in the virgin's womb
and put it off on the cross and tomb
to be worshipped by the church of Rome.
I'm sure this Jesus will not do
either for Englishman or Jew.

§

§

Did Jesus teach doubt? Or did he
give any lessons of philosophy,
charge visionaries with deceiving,
or call men wise for not believing?

§

§

Was Jesus born of a virgin pure
with narrow soul and looks demure?
If he intended to take on sin
the mother should an harlot been,
just such a one as Magdalen
with seven devils in her pen;
or were Jew virgins still more cursed,
and more sucking devils nursed?
Or what was it which he took on
that he might bring salvation?
A body subject to be tempted,
from neither pain nor grief exempted?
Or such a body as might not feel
the passions that with sinners deal?
Yes, but they say he never fell.
Ask Caiaphas; for he can tell.

He mocked the Sabbath, and he mocked
the Sabbath's god, and he unlocked
the evil spirits from their shrines,
and turned fishers to divines;
overturned the tent of secret sins,
and its golden cords and pins.
'Tis the bloody shrine of war
pinned around from star to star,
halls of justice, hating vice,
where the devil combs his lice.
He turned the devils into swine
that he might tempt the Jews to dine;
since which, a pig has got a look
that for a Jew may be mistook.
"Obey your parents."—What says he?
"Woman, what have I to do with you?

No Earthly Parents I confess:
I am doing my Father's business."
He scorned Earth's parents, scorned Earth's god,
and mocked the one and the other's rod.
His seventy disciples sent
against religion and government;
they by the sword of justice fell
and him their cruel murderer tell.
He left his father's trade to roam
a wandering vagrant without home;
and thus he others' labor stole
that he might live above control.
The publicans and harlots he
selected for his company,
and from the adultress turned away
God's righteous law, that lost its prey.

§

§

Do what you will, this life's a fiction
and is made up of contradiction.

§

THERE IS NO NATURAL RELIGION

A

THE ARGUMENT: Humanity has no notion of
moral fitness but from Education. Naturally one
is only a natural organ subject to Sense.

> I. Humanity cannot naturally Perceive, but
> through one's natural or bodily organs.

> II. Humanity by reasoning power can only
> compare and judge of what one has
> already perceived.

> III. From a perception of only three senses
> or three elements none could deduce a
> fourth or fifth.

> IV. None could have other than natural or
> organic thoughts if one had none but
> organic perceptions.

V. Humanity's desires are limited by one's
   perceptions; none can desire what has
   not been perceived.

VI. The desires and perceptions of man
   or woman untaught by anything but
   organs of sense, must be limited to
   objects of sense.

CONCLUSION: If it were not for the poetic
or prophetic character, the philosophic and
experimental would soon be at the ratio of all
things, and stand still unable to do other than
repeat the same dull round over again.

B

I. Human perceptions are not bounded by
   organs of perception; one perceives
   more than sense (though ever so
   acute) can discover.

II. Reason, or the ratio of all we have al-
   ready known, is not the same that it
   shall be when we know more.

III. The bounded is loathed by its possessor. The same dull round even of a universe would soon become a mill with complicated wheels.

IV. If the many become the same as the few when possessed, More! More! is the cry of a mistaken soul, less than all cannot satisfy Humanity.

V. If any could desire what one is incapable of possessing, despair must be one's eternal lot.

VI. The desire of Humanity being infinite the possession is infinite and oneself infinite.

APPLICATION: One who sees the infinite in all things sees God. A man who sees the ratio only sees himself only.

Therefore God becomes as we are, that we may be as He is.

ALL RELIGIONS ARE ONE

The Voice of one crying in the Wilderness

THE ARGUMENT. As the true method of knowledge is experiment the true faculty of knowing must be the faculty which experiences. This faculty I treat of.

PRINCIPLE 1   That the poetic genius is the true humanity; and that the body or outward form of human beings is derived from the poetic genius. Likewise that the forms of all things are derived from their genius, which by the ancients was called an angel and spirit and demon.

PRINCIPLE 2   As all humans are alike in outward form, so (and with the same infinite variety) all are alike in the poetic genius.

PRINCIPLE 3   No man can think write or speak from

his heart, but must intend truth. Thus all
sects of philosophy are from the poetic genius
adapted to the weaknesses of every individual.

Principle 4   As none by travelling over known
lands can find out the unknown; So from
already acquired knowledge human beings
could not acquire more; therefore an universal
poetic genius exists.

Principle 5   The religions of all nations are derived
from each nation's different reception of the
poetic genius which is everywhere called the
spirit of prophecy.

Principle 6   The Jewish and Christian Testaments
are an original derivation from the poetic
genius; this is necessary from the confined
nature of bodily sensation.

Principle 7   As all human beings are alike (though
infinitely various) so all religions and as all
similars have one source.

The true Humanity is the source, he and she being
the poetic genius.

THE MARRIAGE OF HEAVEN AND HELL

THE ARGUMENT

Rintrah roars and shakes his fires in the bur-
    dened air;
hungry clouds swag on the deep.
Once meek, and in a perilous path,
the just man kept his course along
the vale of death.
Roses are planted where thorns grow.
And on the barren heath
sing the honey bees.
Then the perilous path was planted:
and a river, and a spring
on every cliff and tomb;

and on the bleached bones
red clay brought forth.
Till the villain left the paths of ease,
to walk in perilous paths, and drive
the just man into barren climes.
Now the sneaking serpent walks
in mild humility.
And the just man rages in the wilds
where lions roam.
Rintrah roars and shakes his fires in the bur-
    dened air;
hungry clouds swag on the deep.

§

As a new heaven is begun, and it is now thirty-three years since its advent, the eternal Hell revives. And lo! Swedenborg is the angel sitting at the tomb; his writings are the linen clothes folded up. Now is the dominion of Edom, & the return of Adam into Paradise; see Isaiah xxxiv & xxxv chapters:

Without contraries is no progression. Attraction and repulsion, reason and energy, love and hate, are necessary to human existence.

From these contraries spring what the religious call good and evil. Good is the passive that obeys reason. Evil is the active springing from energy.

Good is heaven. Evil is hell.

§

THE VOICE OF THE DEVIL

All Bibles or sacred codes have been the causes of the following errors:

1. That man has two real existing principles, viz: a body and a soul.

2. That energy, called evil, is alone from the body; and that reason, called good, is alone from the soul.

3. That God will torment man in eternity for following his energies.

But the following contraries to these are true:

1. Man has no body distinct from his soul, for that called body is a portion of soul discerned by the five senses, the chief inlets of soul in this age.

2. Energy is the only life and is from the body, and reason is the bound or outward circumference of energy.

3. Energy is eternal delight.

§

Those who restrain desire do so because theirs is weak enough to be restrained; and the restrainer or reason usurps its place and governs the unwilling.

And being restrained it by degrees becomes passive till it is only the shadow of desire.

The history of this is written in *Paradise Lost*, and the governor or reason is called Messiah.

And the original archangel, or possessor of the command of the heavenly host, is called the Devil or Satan, and his children are called Sin and Death.

But in the *Book of Job* Milton's messiah is called Satan.

For this history has been adopted by both parties.

It indeed appeared to reason as if desire was cast out, but the Devil's account is, that the Messiah fell and formed a heaven of what he stole from the Abyss.

This is shown in the Gospel, where he prays to the Father to send the comforter or desire that reason may have ideas to build on, the Jehovah of the Bible being no other than he who dwells in flaming fire. Know that after Christ's death, he became Jehovah.

But in Milton, the father is destiny, the son, a ratio of the five senses, and the holy ghost, vacuum!

Note. The reason Milton wrote in fetters when he wrote of angels and God, and at liberty when of devils and Hell, is because he was a true poet and of the Devil's party without knowing it.

§

A MEMORABLE FANCY

As I was walking among the fires of hell, delighted with the enjoyments of genius, which to angels look like torment and insanity, I collected some of their proverbs: thinking that as the sayings used in a nation mark its character, so the Proverbs of Hell show the nature of infernal wisdom better than any description of buildings or garments.

When I came home, on the abyss of the five senses, where a flat-sided steep frowns over the present world, I saw a mighty devil folded in black clouds, hovering on the sides of the rock; with corroding fires he wrote the following sentence now perceived by the minds of men, and read by them on earth.

How do you know but every bird that cuts the airy way is an immense world of delight, closed by your senses five?

§

PROVERBS OF HELL

In seed time learn, in harvest teach,
in winter enjoy.

Drive your cart and your plow over
the bones of the dead.

The road of excess leads to the palace
of wisdom.

Prudence is a rich ugly old maid
courted by Incapacity.

He who desires but acts not, breeds
pestilence.

The cut worm forgives the plow.

Dip him in the river who loves water.

A fool sees not the same tree that a
wise human sees.

He whose face gives no light, shall
never become a star.

Eternity is in love with the produc-
tions of time.

The busy bee has no time for sorrow.

The hours of folly are measured by
the clock, but of wisdom no clock
can measure.

All wholesome food is caught without
a net or a trap.

Bring out number, weight, and mea-
sure in a year of dearth.

No bird soars too high, if he soars
with his own wings.

A dead body revenges not injuries.

The most sublime act is to set another
before you.

If the fool would persist in his folly,
he would become wise.

Folly is the cloak of knavery. Shame is
pride's cloak.

Prisons are built with stones of law,
brothels with bricks of religion.

The pride of the peacock is the glory
of God.

The lust of the goat is the bounty of
God.

The wrath of the lion is the wisdom
of God.

The nakedness of woman is the work
of God.

Excess of sorrow laughs. Excess of joy
weeps.

The roaring of lions, the howling of
wolves, the raging of the stormy
sea, and the destructive sword, are
portions of eternity too great for
the eye of Man.

The fox condemns the trap, not him-
self.

Joys impregnate. Sorrows bring forth.

Let man wear the fell of the lion,
woman the fleece of the sheep.

The bird a nest, the spider a web,
man friendship.

The selfish smiling fool and the sullen frowning fool shall be both thought wise, that they may be a rod.

What is now proved was once only imagined.

The rat, the mouse, the fox, the rabbit watch the roots; the lion, the tiger, the horse, the elephant watch the fruits.

The cistern contains; the fountain overflows.

One thought fills immensity.

Always be ready to speak your mind, and a base human will avoid you.

Everything possible to be believed is an image of truth.

The eagle never lost so much time as when he submitted to learn of the crow.

The fox provides for himself, but God provides for the lion.

Think in the morning, act in the noon, eat in the evening, sleep in the night.

He who has suffered you to impose on him knows you.

As the plow follows words, so God rewards prayers.

The tigers of wrath are wiser than the horses of instruction.

Expect poison from the standing water.

You never know what is enough unless you know what is more than enough.

Listen to the fool's reproach! it is a kingly title!

The eyes of fire, the nostrils of air, the mouth of water, the beard of earth.

The weak in courage is strong in cunning.

The apple tree never asks the beech how he shall grow, nor the lion the horse how he shall take his prey.

The thankful receiver bears a plentiful harvest.

If others had not been foolish, we should be so.

The soul of sweet delight can never be defiled.

When you see an eagle, you see a portion of genius; lift up your head!

As the caterpillar chooses the fairest leaves to lay her eggs on, so the priest lays his curse on the fairest joys.

To create a little flower is the labor of ages.

Damn braces: Bless relaxes.

The best wine is the oldest, the best
water the newest.

Prayers plow not! Praises reap not!

Joys laugh not! Sorrows weep not!

The head sublime, the heart pathos,
the genitals beauty, the hands and
feet proportion.

As the air to a bird or the sea to a
fish, so is contempt to the con-
temptible.

The crow wished everything was black,
the owl, that everything was white.

Exuberance is beauty.

If the lion was advised by the fox, he
would be cunning.

Improvement makes straight roads, but
the crooked roads without im-
provement are roads of genius.

Sooner murder an infant in its cradle
than nurse unacted desires.

Where man is not, nature is barren.

Truth can never be told so as to be
understood, and not be believed.

Enough! or Too much

The ancient Poets animated all sensible objects with Gods or Geniuses, calling them by the names and adorning them with the properties of woods, rivers, mountains, lakes, cities, nations, and whatever their enlarged and numerous senses could perceive.

And particularly they studied the genius of each city and country, placing it under its mental deity.

Till a system was formed, which some took advantage of and enslaved the vulgar by attempting to realize or abstract the mental deities from their objects; thus began Priesthood.

Choosing forms of worship from poetic tales.

And at length they pronounced that the gods had ordered such things.

Thus men forgot that all deities reside in the human breast.

§

A MEMORABLE FANCY

The Prophets Isaiah and Ezekiel dined with me, and I asked them how they dared so roundly to assert that God spoke to them; and whether they did not think at the time, that they would be misunderstood, and so be the cause of imposition.

Isaiah answered, "I saw no god, nor heard any, in a finite organical perception; but my senses discovered the infinite in everything, and as I was then persuaded, and remain confirmed, that the voice of honest indignation is the voice of God, I cared not for consequences but wrote."

Then I asked: "Does a firm persuasion that a thing is so, make it so?"

He replied, "All poets believe that it does, and in ages of imagination this firm persuasion removed mountains; but many are not capable of a firm persuasion of anything."

Then Ezekiel said, "The philosophy of the east taught the first principles of human perception. Some nations held one principle for the origin and some another; we of Israel taught that the poetic genius (as you now call it) was the first principle and all the others merely derivative, which was the cause of our despising the priests and philosophers of other countries, and prophesying that all gods would at last be proved to originate in ours and to be the tributaries of the poetic genius. It was this that our great poet King David desired so fervently and invokes so pathetically, saying by this he conquers enemies and governs kingdoms. And we so loved our God that we cursed in his name all the deities of surrounding nations, and asserted that they had rebelled. From these opinions the vulgar came to think that all nations would at last be subject to the Jews.

"This," said he, "like all firm persuasions, is come to pass, for all nations believe the Jews' code and worship the Jews' god, and what greater subjection can be?"

I heard this with some wonder, and must confess my own conviction. After dinner I asked Isaiah to favor the world with his lost works. He said none of equal value was lost. Ezekiel said the same of his.

I also asked Isaiah what made him go naked and barefoot three years. He answered, "The same that made our friend Diogenes the Grecian."

I then asked Ezekiel why he ate dung, and lay so long on his right and left side. He answered, "The desire of raising other men into a perception of the infinite. This the North American tribes practise, and is he honest who resists his genius or conscience only for the sake of present ease or gratification?"

§

The ancient tradition that the world will be consumed in fire at the end of six thousand years is true, as I have heard from Hell.

For the cherub with his flaming sword is hereby commanded to leave his guard at tree of life, and when he does, the whole creation will be consumed, and appear infinite and holy, whereas it now appears finite and corrupt.

This will come to pass by an improvement of sensual enjoyment.

But first the notion that man has a body distinct from his soul is to be expunged; this I shall do, by printing in the infernal method, by corrosives, which in Hell are salutary and medicinal, melting apparent surfaces away, and displaying the infinite which was hid.

If the doors of perception were cleansed everything would appear to man as it is, infinite.

For man has closed himself up, till he sees all things through narrow chinks of his cavern.

§

A MEMORABLE FANCY

I was in a printing house in Hell and saw the method in which knowledge is transmitted from generation to generation.

In the first chamber was a dragon-man, clearing away the rubbish from a cave's mouth; within, a number of dragons were hollowing the cave.

In the second chamber was a viper folding round the rock and the cave, and others adorning it with gold, silver, and precious stones.

In the third chamber was an eagle with wings and feathers of air; he caused the inside of the cave to be infinite. Around were numbers of eagle-like men, who built palaces in the immense cliffs.

In the fourth chamber were lions of flaming fire raging around and melting the metals into living fluids.

In the fifth chamber were unnamed forms, which cast the metals into the expanse.

There they were received by men who occupied the sixth chamber, and took the form of books and were arranged in libraries.

The giants who formed this world into its sensual existence and now seem to live in it in chains are in truth the causes of its life and the sources of all activity. But the chains are the cunning of weak and tame minds which have power to resist energy, according to the proverb, "the weak in courage is strong in cunning."

Thus one portion of being, is the prolific; the other, the devouring: to the devourer it seems as if the producer was in his chains, but it is not so; he only takes portions of existence and fancies that the whole.

But the prolific would cease to be prolific unless the devourer as a sea received the excess of his delights.

Some will say, "Is not God alone the prolific?" I answer, "God only acts and is, in existing beings or men."

These two classes of men are always upon earth, and they should be enemies; whoever tries to reconcile them seeks to destroy existence.

Religion is an endeavour to reconcile the two.

Note. Jesus Christ did not wish to unite but to separate them, as in the parable of the sheep and goats! and he says, "I came not to send peace but a sword."

Messiah or Satan or Tempter was formerly thought to be one of the antediluvians who are our energies.

§

A MEMORABLE FANCY

An angel came to me and said, "O pitiable foolish young man! O horrible! O dreadful state! Consider the hot burning dungeon you are preparing for yourself to all eternity, to which you are going in such career."

I said, "Perhaps you will be willing to show me my eternal lot and we will contemplate together upon it and see whether your lot or mine is most desirable."

So he took me through a stable and through a church and down into the church vault at the end of which was a mill: through the mill we went, and came to a cave. Down the winding cavern we groped our tedious way till a void boundless as a nether sky appeared beneath us, and we held by the roots of trees and hung over this immensity. But I said, "If you please, we will commit ourselves to this void, and see whether providence is here also. If you will not I will." But he answered, "Do not presume, O young man, but as we here remain behold thy lot which will soon appear when the darkness passes away."

So I remained with him sitting in the twisted root of an oak. he was suspended in a fungus which hung with the head downward into the deep.

By degrees we beheld the infinite abyss, fiery as the smoke of a burning city. Beneath us at an immense distance was the sun, black but shining. Round it were fiery tracks on which revolved vast spiders, crawling after their prey, which flew or rather swum in the infinite deep, in the most terrific shapes of animals sprung from corruption; and the air was full of them, and seemed composed of them. These are devils and are called powers of the air. I now asked my companion which was my eternal lot? he said, "Between the black and white spiders."

But now, from between the black and white spiders a cloud and fire burst and rolled thro the deep, blackening all beneath, so that the nether deep grew black as a sea and rolled with a terrible noise. Beneath us was nothing now to be seen but a black tempest; till looking east between the clouds and the waves, we saw a cataract of blood mixed with fire and not many stones' throw from us appeared and sunk again the scaly fold of a monstrous serpent. At last to the east, distant about three degrees, appeared a fiery crest above the waves. Slowly it reared like a ridge of golden rocks till we discovered two globes of crimson fire, from which the sea fled away in clouds of smoke. And now we saw, it was the head of Leviathan; his forehead was divided into streaks of green and purple like those on a tiger's forehead; soon we saw his mouth and red gills hang just above the raging foam tinging the black deep with beams of blood, advancing toward us with all the fury of a spiritual existence.

My friend the angel climbed up from his station into the mill. I remained alone, and then this appearance was no more; but I found myself sitting on a pleasant bank beside a river by moonlight hearing a harper who sung to the harp, and his theme was, "The man who never alters his opinion is like standing water, and breeds reptiles of the mind."

But I arose, and sought for the mill, and there I found my angel, who, surprised, asked me how I escaped.

I answered, "All that we saw was owing to your meta-physics: for when you ran away, I found myself on a bank by moonlight hearing a harper. But now we have seen my eternal lot, shall I show you yours?" He laughed at my proposal; but I by force suddenly caught him in my arms, and flew westerly through the night, till we were elevated above the earth's shadow. Then I flung myself with him directly into the body of the sun. Here I clothed myself in white, and taking in my hand Swedenborg's volumes sunk from the glorious clime, and passed all the planets till we came to Saturn. Here I stayed to rest and then leaped into the void between Saturn and the fixed stars.

"Here," said I, "is your lot, in this space, if space it may be called." Soon we saw the stable and the church, and I took him to the altar and opened the Bible, and lo! it was a deep pit, into which I descended driving the angel before me. Soon we saw seven houses of brick, one we entered; in it were a number of monkeys, baboons, and all of that species chained by the middle, grinning and snatching at one another, but withheld by the shortness of their chains. However, I saw that they sometimes grew numerous; and then the weak were caught by the strong and with a grinning aspect, first coupled with and then devoured, by plucking off first one limb and then another till the body was left a helpless trunk. This after grinning and kissing it with seeming fondness they devoured too; and here and there I saw one savorily picking the flesh off of his own tail. As the stench terribly annoyed us both we went into the mill, and I in my hand brought the skeleton of a body, which in the mill was Aristotle's Analytics.

So the angel said: "Your fantasy has imposed upon me and you ought to be ashamed."

I answered: "We impose on one another, and it is but lost time to converse with you whose works are only analytics."

Opposition is true Friendship.

§

I have always found that angels have the vanity to speak of themselves as the only wise; this they do with a confident insolence sprouting from systematic reasoning.

Thus Swedenborg boasts that what he writes is new, though it is only the contents or index of already published books.

A man carried a monkey about for a show, and because he was a little wiser than the monkey, grew vain, and conceived himself as much wiser than seven men. It is so with Swedenborg; he shows the folly of churches and exposes hypocrites, till he imagines that all are religious and himself the single one on earth that ever broke a net.

Now hear a plain fact: Swedenborg has not written one new truth. Now hear another: he has written all the old falsehoods.

And now hear the reason: He conversed with angels who are all religious, and conversed not with devils who all hate religion, for he was incapable through his conceited notions.

Thus Swedenborg's writings are a recapitulation of all superficial opinions, and an analysis of the more sublime, but no further.

Have now another plain fact: Any human of mechanical talents may from the writings of Paracelsus or Jacob Boehme, produce ten thousand volumes of equal value with Swedenborg's. And from those of Dante or Shakespeare, an infinite number.

But when he has done this, let him not say that he knows better than his master, for he only holds a candle in sunshine.

§

A MEMORABLE FANCY

Once I saw a devil in a flame of fire, who arose before an angel that sat on a cloud, and the devil uttered these words:

"The worship of God is: Honoring his gifts in other men, each according to his genius, and loving the greatest men best. Those who envy or calumniate great men hate God, for there is no other God."

The angel hearing this became almost blue, but mastering himself he grew yellow, and at last white, pink and smiling, and then replied,

"Thou idolater, is not God one? and is not he visible in Jesus Christ? and has not Jesus Christ given his sanction to the law of ten commandments and are not all other men fools, sinners, and nothings?"

The devil answered, "Bray a fool in a mortar with wheat,"yet shall not his folly be beaten out of hum. If Jesus Christ is the greatest human, you ought to love him in the greatest degree. Now hear how he has given his sanction to the ten commandments: Did he not mock at the sabbath, and so mock the sabbath's god? murder those who were murdered because of him? turn away the law from the woman taken in adultery? steal the labor of others to support him? bear false witness when he omitted making a defense before Pilate? covet when he prayed for his disciples, and when he bid them shake off the dust of their feet against such as refused to lodge them? I tell you, no virtue can exist without breaking these ten commandments. Jesus was all virtue, and acted from impulse, not from rules."

When he had so spoken, I beheld the angel, who stretched out his arms embracing the flame of fire, and he was consumed and arose as Elijah.

Note. This angel, who is now become a devil, is my particular friend: we often read the Bible together in its infernal or diabolical sense, which the world shall have if they behave well.

I have also: The Bible of Hell, which the world shall have whether they will or no.

One law for the lion and ox is oppression.

§

A SONG OF LIBERTY

1. The Eternal Female groaned! it was heard over all the earth:

2. Albion's coast is sick, silent; the American meadows faint!

3. Shadows of prophecy shiver along by the lakes and the rivers and mutter across the ocean. France, rend down thy dungeon;

4. Golden Spain, burst the barriers of old Rome;

5. Cast thy keys, O Rome, into the deep, down falling, even to eternity down falling,

6. And weep.

7. In her trembling hands she took the newborn terror howling:

8. On those infinite mountains of light, now barred out by the Atlantic sea, the newborn fire stood before the starry king!

9. Flagged with grey browed snows and thunderous visages the jealous wings waved over the deep.

10. The speary hand burned aloft, unbuckled was the shield, forth went the hand of jealousy among the flaming hair, and hurled the newborn wonder through the starry night.

11. The fire, the fire, is falling!

12. Look up! look up! O citizen of London, enlarge your countenance! O Jew, leave counting gold! return to your oil and wine. O African! black African! (go, winged thought, widen his forehead.)

13. The fiery limbs, the flaming hair, shot like the sinking sun into the western sea.

14. Waked from his eternal sleep, the hoary element roaring fled away:

15. Down rushed, beating his wings in vain, the jealous king; his grey browed counsellors, thunderous warriors, curled veterans, among helms, and shields, and chariots, horses, elephants, banners, castles, slings and rocks.

16. Falling, rushing, ruining! buried in the ruins, on Urthona's dens.

17. All night beneath the ruins; then, their sullen flames faded, emerge round the gloomy king.

18. With thunder and fire, leading his starry hosts through the waste wilderness, he promulgates his ten commands, glancing his beamy eyelids over the deep in dark dismay,

19. Where the son of fire in his eastern cloud, while the morning plumes her golden breast,

20. Spurning the clouds written with curses, stamps the stony law to dust, loosing the eternal horses from the dens of night, crying: "Empire is no more! and now the lion and wolf shall cease."

§

CHORUS

Let the priests of the raven of dawn, no longer in deadly black, with hoarse note curse the sons of joy. Nor his accepted brethren whom, tyrant, he calls free; lay the bound or build the roof. Nor pale religious lechery call that virginity, that wishes but acts not!

For everything that lives is holy.

§